Poems, Written and Painted

Poems, Written and Painted

Anders C. Shafer

ISBN: 978-1-958150-31-3
Poems, Written and Painted

Cover image: *Parade from the Pope's Zoo*, a variation on a work included in the book *The Fantastic Journey of Pieter Bruegel* by Anders C. Shafer

Published by **Inner Peace Press**
Eau Claire, Wisconsin, USA
www.innerpeacepress.com

Table of Contents

Poems, Written and Painted

Most of my time is spent happily drawing and painting, but I have a deep, sometimes buried, interest in poetry. Poems make an entrance, in my mind, for mysterious reasons, at unexpected times.

Written between 1966 and 2023, these poems reflect changing convictions of "what's cool."

The collection starts with a few poems I wrote in George Starbuck's "Under-Graduate Poetry Workshop" that I attended during my last semester at the University of Iowa. The book cover is an illustration from my children's book *The Fantastic Journey of Pieter Bruegel*, edited by Donna Brooks, Dutton Children's Books, NYC. My MFA in painting is from Robert Knipschild, University of Cincinnati.

Days will find me in a studio next to my wife Barbara's space in a converted rubber tire factory that sits on the Eau Claire River.

I am a retired "Max Schoenfeld distinguished Professor" from the University of Wisconsin–Eau Claire, where I taught Visual Art for 43 years.

For me, writing poetry seems very similar to making visual art. I think of my paintings as painted poems. In this book, I put in a selection of paintings to illustrate this point. They seem to come from the same mysterious place. Someone said that poems are like "a stream of consciousness set to music." Interesting how the pictures and poems work together.

Troop Train

Two girls hear a train coming through the north woods and run to the station. They find a troop train.

When I Was Born

When I was born in summer
Under a thousand cotton clouds
In a pink plastic breath of air
Full as a sausage in Ohio.

Every minute there were trains
Rattling over warm ties and granite beds
Rocking the town with unseen motion
Heading for the War.

Where bombs were swarming
From silver sparkling airplanes
And toy towns were crumbling
Into lead gingerbread
In France.

Where a woman, twisting microscopically
In the blasting heat, whining splinters,
Emitted my first contemporary
Frozen in death.

Written in Bucyrus, Ohio, Spring 1966

It is confusing yes, somewhat wonderfully, to be
Here drinking in this house where I was born
Where long ago soldiers woke to leggings and mustachios
Went up in blimps or entered ships
To loop the great empty, neutral terriers unafraid,
Returned to all the clanging spoons and peanuts,
Returned in straws to as always kiss soapy breasts
In summer, dreaming Chinas, Castiles, or embarkation Baltimores,
In these rooms where I myself remember Baltimores
Clippering in dreams on hot blue seas over tumbling shells
But the flags are furled,
With the mechanical girls, the rowing houses the
barnacles made of Atlantic,
And the sailors and soldiers were conned by Cleveland
When they woke to talcum and ties.

It is confusing to be here drinking in this house
Where the men came back melancholy in derbies
To wind old victrolas,
To build Harding's tomb, his round, round tomb
To sit around, sit around, wake to sleep
Or motor off to blunders and dust,
Until they fell to the one way questions, until too many fell
Around these rooms where I too remember F.D.R.
Skippering in dreams the great moronic.
But the spades are shelved
With the crackling shacks, the garnished sun,
the steel rimmed politicos.

And the sons of soldiers were bugled away
To wake to gaze on a breach.
It is confusing yes here with all these pictures
Dancing like pistons of tanks the sons slid into
Tanks screaming in streets where some ran burping
Their blood that is called my blood,
And some sat safe with their chevrons shining
But their stomachs ruined.
The men sat silent
And the women walked in and out, in and out
Of these rooms,
Where my remembering began and now goes on
While jets abound booming taller, taller blunders
And I wake anxious in the night.

Boot Camp

When developing the idea of "sequence art," I thought of doing stories that would be in the minds of millions. People probably had the story of the soldier who goes to boot camp, home, then off to die.

Each of the six parts of the story is in sections surrounded or framed by a related image that has a different style and color. Santa Claus appears in the fourth image; the reindeer turn into the dogs of war.

Children of Europe

I lived in Paris in 1950 and attended a French School. The other children were smaller than me. A year ago I was pleased to walk by some French teenagers who were a foot taller than me.

A Short History of American Boxing

Boxcars bang, bundle, beating steel cracking and screaming. They are thick in grit in Colorado. The engineer is called "the butcher." He has knifed his train through the mountains and blasted it out into the plains as if he had no bones to riddle. The brakeman has a blackjack. He is lean and pocked and moves down the stopped train listening in cars. He jerks a door open. Dempsey lifts his teeth to the glare. His eyes are dull and red. He does not speak and backs his punches with all his body. The "butcher" cranes around to see Dempsey looming over his friend and shudders. Dempsey turns away and forgets.

Years later, when asked to construct a metaphor for his punch, Dempsey began to think of babies falling from high windows to knock him cold, then the engineer's face.

A great yellow Buick is looping around dunes and chasing crabs in Delaware. Tall, pale men are standing up still in the waves to watch the car pass them. All day the car has been coming up the coast on the sands. It is steaming from under its hood and its wheels and doors are soaked with salt.

It is night along the Atlantic. The great car has stopped. Jack Johnson is lying in the back seat drinking whiskey. He does not smile. He is not a tragic figure. Around him in Delaware a thousand old stogies smolder in the dark and round fat men guffaw, guffaw.

Joe, Joe Pazooka. Who were you anyway? Some young ad man's dream? Some strong, clean imagined cartoon in deepest Pittsburg? Though alien to most of your kind of Kingdom, I cannot lower my thumb to you, to bubblegum, to the hilarious pop of your punches. I cannot because I remember the vacant boys in Saturday stadiums, who are pure as Wheaties dreams, flattening your fruity sugars on their tongues. I cannot because I remember the saucy girls in swimming sun, blimping your spheres from their lips, yearning for the silliness of your collapse. Some nasty guy breathing your soft stickiness in a frightened face. Then the pimply kid loading your machines in Chicago while the custodian with bent legs scraps you out of the dark under a bench. Joe, Joe Pazzoka, the dentist's best friend.

Fall and Rise of Cincinnati

Cincinnati, from 1966-68, was a rough place to live, but I loved the city. The images are from memories of Vine Street, for instance, mixed with places at different times of history, references to Art History, so there is no "now" or "then," but time is mixed as in memory.

15

Performing Elephant

I painted a small blob landscape when we went home for the pandemic. It looked like a circus wagon with an elephant painted by Rembrandt, maybe drunk. I painted it that way and it led to a series on elephants and Rembrandts. A friend sent me a detail of a Rembrandt print that contained a tiny elephant.

I work by synthesizing ideas.

The District of Columbia

In a time stopped now forever in my mind, we roll in a heavy, black car out of the scorpion days of Arkansas into the spell of the city in summer, into the District of Columbia in 1953.

When you come out of the heat there is a coolness in the monuments.

As the slow streetcars glide like metal bugs down the hill at Georgetown, planes circle in over the Atlantic, over Antietam, over Arlington. At Griffith Stadium the afternoon crowd murmurs under their cloud of smoke, a small white ball rises out into the sun.

Up in the domes, through the Greek columns, you see the blurred light of a paradise.

In the contented, fat bulge of a dark echoing civilization, the ancient Ms. Nicolay goes down through the flowers of the Kennedy Warren Hotel to tea. The armed entourage of Dwight David Eisenhower, smiling from his window, is speeding in down the shaded avenues from Burning Tree.

The fountains echo in the dust.

In his grey room, a cold powerful man leans back heavily, silent for a moment under the crush of time. Long before the Uzis and needles of present time, pajama man quarter man, the human flag, pass among homeless people laughing bitterly in the steaming heat of 14th Street, of Dupont Circle.

Outside, the damp earth is thick in boxwood, honeysuckle, a gentle hot richness of life.

Later, I stand. A small boy without a shirt in the approaching evening. Men of granite speak to me. "The ways of the world are locked in place and we must follow them into oblivion."

I do not believe it.

Christmas Time

"I'll be home for Christmas," sang the sailors,
Tripping down the ship stairs,
"So, go kiss the moon."
The dark sea thunders under the big wind.
"I'll be home for Christmas," sang the whistling man,
"Soap behind my ears, a crisp, white shirt.
I can almost reach the moon."
The small dog barks happily under giant elm trees.
"Pink wine and gravy," said the old woman
Over the snow filled birdbath.
"You could just hug the moon."
The smell of apples lingers over the back steps, in the vestibule.
"Son of a gun," sang the old train,
"I'm tired. Lay me out in rusty pieces in the meadow
And let the snow fly over me,
The children roll and dance."
"No," said the conductor. "It's Christmas.
One more trip.
It's Christmas and the bells and swinging lights
Snow over the headlamps in 1943, 1955, 1965,
All those years, time and again
The same thing.
Go up the mountain line and kiss the moon."
The old train went on but said,
"We are the melting snow that kisses the moon."

One Fine Evening In The World

Years ago, getting off a train in Providence, Rhode Island, after several days in the big cities, in summer, I heard the conductor say to an elderly woman, "It's a beautiful evening." This is how it felt.

Elegy to the 20th Century

Folds of the tent drift open,
A girl, flickering sparrow,
Reaches up to straighten her hair,
Then cuts a path through the weeds
To the 20th Century.
Buffalo Bill sits back in the shade.
His teeth are worn and yellow.

Sun on the ripening fields,
The fragrant air
Carries Chopin
A romance turning
Into the smoking sky
Over shocked eyes.

Delicate as a shell in the waves,
The elegant ship
Floats by thin, white buildings,
Carries people like pictures of people,
Laughing and chattering,
Drops of gin falling on mahogany.

Rubber burns beside the road.
A long curling ribbon from east Texas, through Oklahoma.
In the black air a boy dreams of Hollywood,
Starlets ascending from buses into drugstores,
Paper in the wind of a freight train
Going away to California.

My mother leans from her window
In Sam Houston Gardens.
Looking up into the sky
She thinks she hears deep notes on a piano
Held for hours.
Claude Edderly relives his dream,
A blue-green, uncharred paradise,
Cypress Gardens under little clouds in Florida.
"Now I have become death."

Theaters of children watch
Reruns of the Engola Gay
Taking off, over and over.
Now the air is filled with joking salesman.
My grandfather's yard dreams of the white bench,
Of people dropping by on a summer night,
Catching fireflies.
Out on the Interstate
A man grips his wheel
Fighting sleep.

The Shirt-Waist or Triangle Fire 1911

I took the route used to dispose of the bodies from near Washington Square to down by the Hudson. I saw this picture as a monument to the women lost a century ago.

A Trip To Cleveland

My grandfather and I took trips to Cleveland. I mix real memory with history.

North Central Ohio

In Crestline now the small dead speak
Huddled in the vestibules of paradise.
"Remember me, remember me."
"Where you walked with your million stories?"
The ancient street yawns, empty.
Back porches settle into infinite dust,
Ground over and over.
A child's face flashes in the sun,
Through the shade of pine trees,
Like my grandfather's voice fading
On a wobbly tape.

In April 1865, when Lincoln died
Men gathered around and said,
"Now he belongs to the ages."
His small train passed through the deep woods
Into the night, while storms crossed the land,
Roaring over the leaning trestles,
Past the longer trains,
Leaving dry cinders mixing on the roadbeds
In Crestline.
Mind to wind and water,
How shall we be remembered?

Some Time Ago in Wisconsin

Some time ago in Wisconsin,
After the War,
It was winter again.
A young man stepped off his train.
The trees bent down in the snow.
People were shut tightly in their houses,
Frying fish from the summer.
The newspaper had predicted a quiet night
Over the cold fields
In the little one light towns
Sitting in a great, beautiful space
Under the moon.
Coming in, a gulp of air
Turned to gentle steam,
Rolling into the furnace heat,
The loving warmth of bodies, blankets, and sleep.

The Lost Dog

People post pictures of lost animals on a pole by my house. I can never find out if they were found or not. A metaphor?

Jack Cole

Cartoonist Jack Cole invented the "Plastic Man" character. He could stretch any part of his body to do in bad guys. I use Jack to depict the frantic life of an illustrator. He worked in Chicago—Hugh Hefner....

Drunken Man Walking Home at 11:15 a.m.

The drunken man walks into a whirlwind of nothing at 11:15 a.m. He is going toward home but steps seemingly backwards, sideways. Maybe he will collapse into a pile of bones and fat. Waves are in his body, a choppy lake of beer and vodka, up inside his chest, down. Cars, other men, go by, driven inevitably toward work, tailgating, gritty, squinting. The drunken man sways like a dying top, his arms flailing to catch something other than air. Then, a frustrating quietness, rolling in emptiness, a ship turning almost upside down in a giant wave. The old machine drops a spinning nut down the stained floor, disappearing, going nowhere, lost. He stops, pulled backwards into an ocean of trees and light. The cement walk snakes up.

Home, a hard rectangle of cigarette smoke, screams, musty blankets, couch like sharp whiskers, stinking breath, some kind of vast, violent sleep.

Troop Trains: My Mother's Dream

Her dream; as she tells it, driving at night, the fifteen miles to Crestline, with my father's parents, driving because the troop trains are coming, then waiting in the coal smoke, feeling the familiar cold numbness in her feet. The loud rows of dark, brown passenger cars suddenly begin to appear, speeding by every eight minutes. She waves a white handkerchief... Someone waves back through the steamed up window. "Not him," yells my grandfather. "We won't see our son."

When she tells me about this dream of another time, I sense that she is talking about my sister and me, as we sit in the emptiness of her small room, and maybe it wasn't a dream.

Stilwell

Joseph Stilwell (1883-1946) was an American General who worked in China and Burma during WWII. He recorded things he saw on his long walks, including a three-thousand-year-old water clock and, from a river boat, the body of a man with his son tied to him, floating past.

Sad Poem

I took a walk on a summer day
By the quiet stadium
When life was everlasting.
A breeze came over the river
Under the weeping trees
Carrying winter
Which was far away
But always near
In life everlasting.

No Longer

The gaunt skeleton of the Dean declares:
"Now there shall be no more football,
No more cracked heads,
Mouths full of dirt and grass,
On a cold fall afternoon.
All inflated leather,
Pointed egg shapes, shell like, oval sort of things,
Shall be deflated and destroyed.
The laughter of big men shall be quelled
And also buried in this cemetery,
Next to the wealthy corpses,
With bigger stones."

Rembrandt's Honeymoon

Rembrandt takes his second wife on a walking tour of the Netherlands and wakes up happy.

The History of Futurism

A school of Italian artists who embraced motion and, for some reason, chaos and violence?

How the Sun Fills the Room

In this northern winter day
The light that fills the room
With window shapes
Is cold, immaculate, pure
As angels in a Renaissance painting
Riding the beams of Maggiore
Over the thick, collapsing treasure.
Shadows of steam speed south
Developing, then imploding like the ocean.
Perhaps we will come out
Of a long dark tunnel.
The discomfort of sitting suddenly lifted
By smashing light at the end.
Light as joyous as "Paradise,"
Or "just spring,"
Still, three months out.

Silent Cal

One fine evening in the world,
Between the Wars
There was a gentle warmth
In all the villages and cities.

The fields were filled with corn and wheat
Waiting for the harvest
And farmers could rest on the porch
After their hot meals and dream.

Looking out into the many colors in the sky,
As the sun began to go down
The stars to show, the moon to glow
Flickering on the White House windows.

People grew quiet in their happiness,
Buses and trains slowed down in the cities,
Crowds coming out of them stopped
Looking up in awe at the beautiful sky.

Silent Cal, in his light grey suit
Sat up straight
Watching a dark bird
Drift over the mall
A piercing light flooded the bank door
As a man walked to lock it
And children closed dry butterflies
In a box.

Near Durand

The Riverboat Gang

My father gave me a photograph he had taken, over a hundred years ago, of a gang of river boys fighting for a dime.

Working in America

1964. I am painting a hawk on a sign in Iowa, a sign that will fall flat into the prairie grass, the black, yellow, and orange disintegrating into the pale ochre of clay. I am painting to buy something disposable; deep fried chicken, chocolate pie, whole milk, and coffee.

The boss drives by in an extinct pink and black Mercury coup, and excited by my (not really) artistry, drives aimlessly into the mud, sinking up to his out of date latches and is stuck inside, due to too many disposables; four over easy, white toast, American fries, and a box of mixed donuts for the back seat.

A nearby farmer on a rusty diesel tractor pulling a manure spreader to make something high fructose makes a sort of circle of the story.

Two days after the farmer pulls him out, the boss sends a man with a pistol, who will soon die, to my room, with a fifty dollar bill and a bottle of Four Star Hennesey Cognac, which in the hands of a nineteen-year-old painter, will be instantly disposable.

Meanwhile, in Italy, a contemporary ladles globs of mortar into the top of a ninth century bridge, then goes home with his pay to eat canned tuna mixed with tomato paste and pasta and has bottled water flat as eternity.

Assassination Attempt of President Truman

Minneapolis

It seems elegant in summer
This park by the museum with the Rembrandt,
Yet a man lies on a hill,
Unapproachable as a dog lying in a blue-black shadow.
Perhaps he will jump up,
Birds will swarm over the street.

Two policemen slouch low in their car.
They smoke and stare at the man.
They could throw him like a candy wrapper
In the back seat, whaling with their sticks.

He does not move.
They drive away.
Night begins to shroud the park.

Then, the man lies erased from history.
The child, who has appeared like this
For centuries, runs away,
Between the heavy houses
By the side of the park
Before the stars and moon
Take their natural configuration
And the police come back to form a line
To place his body in a wagon.

Gorky

Gorky escaped the Armenian Holocaust and came to America to become one of the world's great artists, mixing cultures and styles.

Fayetteville

Rain and more rain stains the grey house in the hill, behind the pines, beyond the burnt field. "Jesus loves me, this I know." Two little girls, shivering by the locked door, keep turning the knob, singing.

A corner store sleeps in the evening heat. Kids come in with empty coke and orange drink bottles to trade for pennies. Small white boxes of sugar crystals, labeled with a blue boy in a cowboy hat riding a miniature mountain, are stacked next to wax lips, orange spongey peanuts. My father stops in for cigarettes and turns to gaze into the backyard. There, in the shade of magnolias, people in overalls and calico are biting into watermelon. My father is down from the Pentagon for a job interview to teach History to college students. His mind is weary from Hiroshima and Nagasaki. He lights a Lucky Strike and decides to move to Fayetteville, Arkansas, to the end of nowhere. 1947.

Mrs. Wilson had a hen house on the side of a clay hill that was thick with caterpillar nests, walking sticks, and milkweed. The wood on the hen house was patched with torn tarpaper and linoleum. For the most part, the chickens sat back in their dark brown roosts and didn't peck when you reached for the egg. Though she seemed lonely and loving, Mrs. Wilson was convinced that when her flagstone cottage went up in the last judgment, I would go down in the conflagration, and she, I guess, would go up to a place that was shiny and white. In the book *The Family of Man* there is a photograph of an elderly woman who looks like Mrs. Wilson. The caption reads: "I am alone with the beating of my heart."

At Age Two I Wandered Away From Home

My father appears as a soldier
And whistles
Like a bird,
But I am gone.
The empty stage turns dark
Walled by a backdrop of dull apartments,
Where I live, in memory, as a child,
When I had no place to go,
But wandered into an urban woods
Now gliding away
On the theater of an old lake,
Toward the river.
Fisherman hold up their catch
As I pass.

"Any luck?" "Not much."
In his book, Orhan Pamuk
Hears a muffled roar
Through his apartment window
On the Bosporus, at midnight
And sees a giant dark shape
Pass, a Russian battle ship
Fading through the Golden Horn
Beamed in, over the waves
Directly down the buzzing lane of light
Into eternity.

At a different time
The goats, this way or that
Followed by their wobbly shepherd.
A wild dog scatters the shaggy cows
Into the woods,
To be found as I was found,
They, nonchalantly eating grass,
Me, two miles from the apartments,
Throwing my shoes into the stream.

Wandering Away From Home

This work is about the poem—me wandering away from home. It was by the Pentagon in Washington.

Marie Antoinette

She starts out as a doll then becomes real as reality takes over.

Washington D.C.-Spring

Spring.
Chaotic clouds of birds fly
Over dark green oceans.
In Washington, the sun sinks below
The river trees
Like an eternal ship rolling
Into the forever universe
And long ago, mostly forgotten,
The delicate poet, seducer, E. E. Cummings
Sits at a table in a pool of faint light
To read:
"in just
spring when the world is mud-
luscious the little
lame balloon man
whistles far and wee...."

I lean back, feeling my shampooed hair
My clean pressed shirt.
Then, we leave, a slow train coming
Out of the long stuffy tunnel of winter
On to the damp sidewalks of the night
And all the buds and blossoms
And Shakespeare suggest:
It is the time for love.

The House on First Avenue

On First Avenue, Eau Claire, Wisconsin, near a rusty railroad bridge that crossed the Chippewa River, there was an "American Four Square" house, painted white. Now-defunct lumber mills had been visible across the river due to area of open water that gave off towering clouds of steam in the winter. Logs could be trapped and sawn into shingle or boards to be bumped south toward the Mississippi. I, a good number of small animals in the area, and my young family lived there in the 1970s.

During this time islands of caramelized looking foam floated in the Chippewa's currents. A biology Professor from the local University was often spotted hauling buckets of river water to his lab. His shocking analysis forced the State of Wisconsin to order treatment.

On one warm spring afternoon a large male cat came sauntering down the back alley and turned into our back yard. He began to cry, then was met with loving hands and a dish of leftover herring in a pearly cream sauce and decided to stay for life. The small animals that inhabited our house soon disappeared. No more wall mirrors screaming at me while I combed my hair. One of my daughters named him Peter after a friend she missed. He slept upstairs in a rug bed. But, one early winter day, forgetting he had been neutered, he left. We thought it might be forever. Yet, much later, on a sub-zero February night a stranger rang the doorbell and loudly announced: "I have your cat," as Peter walked casually between my legs and went up to his bed. He stayed until he crawled up on our porch to die after being struck in the dark by a car.

The other houses in the neighborhood were built mostly during the lumbering years. Metal siding had begun to appear, though, as with our place, the old wood showed many winters. To set a stage, through the picture windows, over the front porch, across the water was the confluence of the Chippewa with the smaller Eau Claire River. You could see the richly shaded banks of the Eau Claire where bands of mud-spattered, wild eyed boys on "dirt bikes" seemed to be constantly, recklessly weaving around elderly fishermen. One could see remnants of Northern States Power warehouses, the abandoned Phoenix Steel plant where treads had been made for tanks in the World Wars. Off to the side of the railroad tracks, next to the bridge, there was a teetering boxcar into which hundreds of rotting tires, ages unknown, had been tossed. If this was dumpy, I didn't notice. I was preoccupied with life and this was home.

But then, fate decided that the house should be painted. I asked around for the best paint. It was "Cook." I bought several gallons. When you tell people you are going to paint your house you will hear: "You have to scrape it down to the bare wood." A friend had purchased a scraper that heated and almost burned his house down. I hosed the walls, shaved off the peeling chips and using the old paint as a "primer," turned the house "new." It stayed that way for decades.

During one of those beautiful Wisconsin days with a high wind from the northwest and cumulus clouds, some of the "wild boys" set the boxcar filled with tires on fire. A plume of grey smoke rolled across the Chippewa, on to the side of my white house and it was soon two-toned. I shrugged, hosed off the tire soot, and repainted in a day. I was young then.

After a shooting and a fire in a house across the alley (according to legend, it had floated down, in a flood, from the town of Chippewa Falls, to land in that spot), we moved.

I miss watching the stages of the churning Chippewa, which had seemed in tune with the flow of humanity, in cars and trucks, on First Avenue, which is now a quiet foot path. The house is pink.

Elegy to the Lost Artists of Eau Claire, Wisconsin

"There is nothing new in this town
You should be more up to date."
Said the visiting critic.
He didn't understand the songs of artists
Who had been to the dark places of the heart,
Seen the water curl endlessly to the shore,
Sitting in little houses, minds soaring
Like crying birds across the world,
Landing, flying away without reason.

I passed a man I knew was dead,
Walking in the snowy haze,
Flakes falling into the river and the road,
I thought I heard him say,
"I am asleep in eternity,
The wind blows empty in my presence.
All that is left of me is my Art."
Soon I was alone again,
The emptiness on either side,
An impossible silence.
Snow fell until evening,
Significant accumulations were reported.

Victorian Child

I saw a movie, years ago, about a homeless child in London who found a Queen Victoria coin. He fell in love with the image on the coin and found a way to see her. In this story, the child is discovered by a beautiful upper-class girl who attempts to nurse him but fails...

51

Eau Claire, Wisconsin

Two rivers rolled
Through great pine forests.
People came, savaging an ancient world,
Building where the ice broke,
Fire smoke mixing with winter steam,
Rising between trees falling
Into fast, heavy water.

Still through the mud clouds
Came shining fish.
You could see them leave,
Passing the sawdust piled high,
That seemed to hold the town.

After the last logs bumped south
Toward the Mississippi
Fishermen, entering the confluence,
Stood up, shocked by silence,
As the saws shut down forever.

A hundred stark winters fade away
Eau Claire lies ringed by shells
Of motels, car washes, malls,
Black paint on door windows
Peels away, the many names replaced or gone.

I see Eau Claire one summer night
Walking down the hill from the hospital
Lit up like a toy town,
Resting by the old river.
Earlier, raking leaves around the garage,
I had found snow,
Then something like sawdust.

Later, I walked with my daughters
On the rusty railroad bridge.
There was a high wind from the northwest,
Scattered showers.
"Why are you holding our hands so tight?"

Lynn Dance Company

For decades I enjoyed attending dance concerts at Chalice Stream Studios in Ladysmith, Wisconsin. Barry Lynn, Michael Duran, and a company of dancers, including my wife Barbara, created a magic spell that felt like "A Thousand and One Nights." This was in an old school house that had been moved.

Fire

My great grandfather was the fire chief of a county in Ohio. He drove a steamer behind great horses.

Cultural Origins

I am walking past Chevyland,
Wisconsin Avenue, Bethesda Maryland.
A man is pin-stripping,
"I love you Rose,"
On a blue Chevrolet
That carries heavy chrome.
The culture is closed,
Button down, urban, well-to-do.
A bedroom community,
Television, Jim Beam, Cutty Sark, gasoline,
Terror.

Two Similar Migrations: Variation on a Painting by Watteau

Aristocrats of the 17th Century
Are departing,
In a kind of minuet,
From the Isle of Love (Cythera).
Boarding a strange golden boat,
They leave their fragile, isolated world,
Perhaps for the future,
Perhaps beyond love.
Watteau, buried below his creation,
Will never know.

Watteau's Heart

I've had a life-long fascination with Antoine Watteau, the great French Rococo painter who was also a sign painter.

Old Man Filled With Sorrow

My Grandfather and Me

I am my wallet, my coins,
And a stick of chewing gum,
A fishing box and yellow rod.
I push the boat, making it glide
On the quiet lake.
Leaning over I can see the bottom.
A small fish disappears into a hole.

Study for the Broken and Stolen Boat

Years ago, an old man rented sailboats for children by the pool of the Luxembourg Gardens, Paris. I was there in 1950 so can only remember parts of the real story. A boy broke No. 16, causing a riot. I invented the next part. The boy throws the boat into the Seine when, some time later, it is found and repaired by chipmunks. They sail it off to sea.

Anders C. Shafer is an Emeritus Professor at the University of Wisconsin–Eau Claire, where he was the Max Schoenfeld Distinguished Professor. He taught painting, drawing, and illustration for 43 years.

A practicing professional artist, he has works in many museums including: The Smithsonian, the Allen Museum, Portland Museum of Art, and the Sheldon Museum. He has won over a hundred awards and been in countless exhibitions. His best known book is *The Fantastic Journey of Pieter Bruegel*, published by Dutton's Children's Books, New York.

Painting by Barbara Shafer

www.ingramcontent.com/pod-product-compliance
Lightning Source LLC
Chambersburg PA
CBHW041430120626
46547CB00002B/158